GW00372182

Pictures From The
GARDEN

Winter landscape, near Sally Gap

LIAM BLAKE

Pictures From The
G A R D E N

A Portrait of Wicklow

Introduction by
DAVID PRITCHARD

For Sahoko

First published in 1999 by Real Ireland Design Limited ©.
27 Beechwood Close, Boghall Road, Bray, Co. Wicklow, Ireland.
Telephone: + 353 1 2860799. Fax: + 353 1 2829962.

Photography © Liam Blake.

Introduction by David Pritchard.

Book & jacket design Brian Murphy.

British Library Cataloguing in Publication Data.
A catalogue record for this book is available from
the British Library

ISBN 0946887128

INTRODUCTION

The photographs in this book will undoubtedly evoke a response both from Wicklow residents and the county's many admirers at home and abroad. Most Dubliners are familiar with their southern neighbour's seaside towns, beaches and mountain fastnesses, whilst beauty spots like Glendalough and the Meeting of the Waters are renowned the world over. These attractions and recreational activities like hill walking and horse riding draw many thousands of visitors annually, but there is more to Wicklow than its function as a giant rural theme park for tourists and day trippers. Geographical factors have conspired to make it the most individualistic and complex county in Leinster, with a historical and cultural heritage that rivals its awesome scenic beauty.

Before writing this introduction to Liam Blake's book I took a look at a map of Wicklow. On one level its mixture of browns, greens, blues and yellows tell all there is to know about the county - that at the centre it has an upland region with high mountains, lakes and deep river valleys; and to the east a green coastal strip edged by a rim of beaches and the blue waters of the Irish sea. The map shows little pine trees spotted about the county - each by my calculation about a thousand feet high - to denote the recently planted coniferous forests which now cover huge swathes of the bogs and hills, whilst at its southernmost edge a few deciduous trees mark the last remnants of Wicklow's oak woods at Coolattin. West of the mountains the level plains of central Ireland stretch away in a monotonous green shade into Carlow and Kildare.

The map's scattered place names and roads give a useful overview of the presence of mankind in the Wicklow landscape. The main settlements are along the coast, with a few market towns and villages along the eastern and western margins of the mountains, but the dark brown interior is clearly empty of habitation. The only exception is the ruined monastic site of Glendalough, which sits almost at the centre of the hills. A few roads cross the uplands in an east to west direction, but for the most part the main routes run north to south on either side of the interior, with a confusing network of yellow minor roads branching off into the valley floors and foothills.

For some reason I find this two-dimensional mapmaker's depiction of Wicklow's rugged terrain and wild coastline conjures up memories of bright summer days spent at Brittas Bay or beside Lough Dan. This is the visionary landscape - suspended in time under a perfectly clear sky - that is Wicklow at its most benign. Even now, driving down to Aughrim on a sunny morning, I find the sight of the humped mountains soaring above the valley's fields and copses uplifting to my spirits. And who would not be moved by curving rainbows that seem to fall to earth beyond the next hedgerow, or by mists rising up the hill slopes to peter out within a few feet from where you sit in bright sunlight? At such moments the face of Wicklow seems almost magical in its clarity, as if god had polished the fields, forests and granite mountains with cosmic beeswax.

Although there are times when Wicklow truly is paradise on earth, anybody planning to visit the county would be well advised to pack an umbrella along with their suntan lotion and camera. Preferably a very big umbrella, since Wicklow weather was not intended for the faint hearted. In fact a rainy day in the hills is an uniquely depressing experience, the climatic equivalent of sitting through a twelve hour long bagpipe concert. If the variegated colours of a map tell 'what the satellite saw' on one of the county's cloudless summer days, they do not capture the gloominess of pine plantations, dull bogs and wet fields beneath slate grey skies - the depressing hues of a bad Wicklow day. This is the other face of the hills - the shadowy cloak of cloud cover that can shroud the outrageous magnificence of Lough Dan or the intimacy of the wooded glens around Enniskerry, where on a clear day every twist of the road brings a fresh view of the hills and mountains.

Wicklow's distinct character has been shaped by the upland wilderness of stunning natural beauty and great geological interest that is its hard granite heart. The U shaped glens, waterfalls and basin lakes of the hills were formed during the Ice Ages of the last two million years, but their granite skeletons are over 400 million years old. They originated when molten material, thrust into older rocks during the collision of the European and American continental plates, slowly cooled into huge bosses of coarse granite. These stone foundations became Time's sculptor's blocks, from which the elements, glaciers and melting water slowly carved the rounded mountains, river gorges and valleys of the uplands.

What makes the Wicklow hills so remarkable is not their size - they rise to a mere 927 metres at the highest point - but rather their accessibility and the wide range of habitats found within a comparatively small area. On one hand, as any hill walker can confirm, the rise and fall of the terrain divides the county up into a maze of nooks and crannies, each with its own geological features and distinct scenic qualities. On the other it is possible to sample Wicklow's gamut of natural and human environments from sea shore to mountain top in a day's comfortable drive. Within a few dozen miles the traveller can journey from the urban sprawl of Bray to the wooded peace of Glendalough or the empty boglands around the Sally Gap.

Wicklow packs so much exquisite scenery in less than two thousand square miles that its human dimension is sometimes overshadowed. Yet for thousands of years the hand of man has changed and moulded the face of the landscape. And from prehistory to the present day each Age has left its monuments, whether passage grave, castle, great house or ornamental garden. The most vivid of these historical reminders are those of the eighteenth and nineteenth centuries, when the woods which covered much of the county had been cleared and the Anglo-Irish landlords were establishing their estates. The great demesne of Powerscourt, with its exquisite gardens and rolling parklands, is the most spectacular relic of this era. More importantly, perhaps, it was the time when the Wicklow countryside was tamed by hedgerows and field systems, and improving landlords founded most of the inland villages, with their neat stone houses, town halls and churches. Nor was the industrial development of the county ignored; ruins at Avoca, Connary and other places mark the sulphur and copper mines which until about 1880 made an important contribution to the local economy.

These activities brought new immigrants into the region, many of whom - for instance the Welsh and Cornish miners brought over to open up the county's ore deposits - were assimilated into the existing population like earlier Gaelic, Viking and Norman settlers before them. In fact all of Wicklow's inhabitants - no matter how rooted in the countryside they seem - descend ultimately from 'blow ins' of one sort or another, whether they arrived as farmers, conquerors or refugees. The county's most common family names confirm these outside origins, most obviously Doyle (from the Irish Dubgall, or 'black foreigner'), which descends from Vikings who settled around Arklow in the tenth century. The prolific O'Tooles and O'Byrnes, in contrast, were respectively the Gaelic rulers of north and south Kildare until the Normans drove them into the hills around 1200.

The militant role of these families in Wicklow's history illustrates the tensions which have existed between the mountainous interior and the adjacent lowlands and coastal areas since the Norman conquest in the late twelfth century. The O'Byrnes were prominent leaders of the native Irish resistance to the English colony in Dublin and Leinster, and from their strongholds at Glenmalure and Castlekevin terrorized the lowlands for centuries until finally being subdued by the armies of Elizabeth I. Due to their tenacious defence of their independence Wicklow was not shired until 1605, becoming almost the last part of Ireland to fall under government control.

A legacy of this resistance was the survival of Wicklow's upland cultural heritage, with its 'longhouse' cottages and other elements more usually associated with the West of Ireland. Eventually the tradition of harbouring rebels and outlaws in the mountains contributed to the taming and dispersal of their inhabitants, for in the aftermath of the 1798 Rebellion the activities of guerilla bands forced the government to build 'military' roads across the interior and place garrisons at Glencree, Glenmalure and other strategic spots. Yet although the nineteenth and twentieth centuries saw rural Wicklow transformed by famine, emigration and agricultural reforms, her people - like those of other mountain cultures - remained notably inward-looking, conservative and resistant to outside influences until recent decades. Even nowadays, when the isolation and poverty that once made Wicklow the Cinderella of Leinster counties have been swept away, the communities in the valleys and countryside retain a notable sense of their local identity.

The coast, with its towns, beaches and eroding cliffs, displays another facet of Wicklow, one that has its own scenic attractions and an impressive maritime tradition. There is the wild beauty of the headlands of Wicklow and Bray, the stony strand at Newcastle and the sand dunes of Brittas Bay - so busy on a summer's day, so empty in winter. Two of the three sizable towns along the coast - Arklow and Wicklow - are Viking foundations whose names derive from old Norse. The Normans raised castles and abbeys at both centres, but the modern towns have only developed over the last three hundred years or so. Arklow is the larger and busier of the two centres, but Wicklow is the more attractive, with its narrow main street and rows of small artisan dwellings. For a long time the town was a pleasant but rather sleepy backwater, but in recent times it has been growing at an extraordinary rate and is now surrounded by new housing estates.

The unprecedented overflow of Dublin's population into the north of

Wicklow is an inevitable consequences of the city's expansion in recent years. The effects of the capital's proximity is most clearly seen around Bray, which has now effectively become one of its satellite towns. Until the late 1960's Bray was a thriving seaside resort, which alongside the amusements and funfairs on its promenade could offer attractions like a cable car ride to the top of the Head and dancing at the Arcadia Ballroom. Over the last thirty years, however, the decline of the town's tourist trade has been paralleled by the building of housing and industrial estates on its outskirts, and it is now part of an almost continuous belt of development which stretches into south county Dublin and beyond.

Wicklow is used to serving Dublin's needs; after all in 1939 the Irish government drowned 6,500 acres of its land around Blessington to provide a reservoir and hydro-electric power station for the city. Nevertheless the potential harm that the present building boom might cause to the county's identity and rural integrity causes some concern. Fortunately these matters do not fall within the scope of this book, and the Wicklow of Liam Blake's photographs is not the glorified garden suburb of the estate agent's advertisement, where a derelict cowshed is 'a potentially desirable residence in need of restoration' and 'less than one hour's drive from Dublin'. Nor is it the quick fix of a day's coach tour offering 'Powerscourt, Glendalough, The Meetings of the Waters and Ballykissangel' - with lunch and two toilet breaks. Rather his images are frozen moments from a wider and more authentic spectrum of Wicklow life, and display their varying subjects with compassion, insight and an artist's eye. Everybody who appreciates the special qualities of Wicklow will enjoy and treasure this pictorial essay.

———————— Winter, Blessington reservoir. ————————

————— Organic sheep farming family, lacken —————

Electricity linesmen, Ballyknockan

The Immaculate Heart House, Grangecon

Woodland, Powerscourt estate

Fishmongers, Bray

———————— Sheep farmer above Roundwood ————————

Military Road to Laragh

Forestry workers Glenmacnass

River Liffey (detail) Coronation plantation

Dune (detail) Brittas bay

The Coronation plantation

Snowfield, Vartry

———————— Sociologist, Greenan ————————

Chemical engineers, I.F.I. plant, Arklow

View towards Lough Dan

Trees and water, Glendalough

Blessington reservoir

———————— Motorcycle dealers, Bray ————————

——————— Harbour Master, Wicklow port ———————

——————— Arklow port ———————

———————— Fishermen, Aughrim river ————————

Ploughing champion, Newcastle

———————— Autumn field, Rathdrum ————————

Broad lough

Abandoned car, Great Sugarloaf mountain

Caretakers, Dwyer Mc Allister cottage, Glen of Imaal

Glen of Imaal Red Cross mountain rescue team

Funfair, Bray Promenade

Maze proprietors, Greenan

Travellers, Rocky Valley

Avonmore river, Clara Vale

——————— Erratic (boulder transported by glacier), Luggala ———————

———————— Winter, Lacken ————————

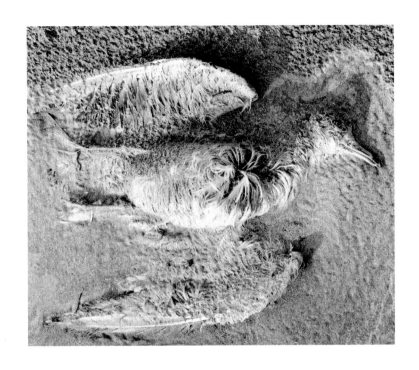

——————— Dead Gull, Brittas bay ———————

Landrover mechanics, Ballinaclash

———————— Spring fields, Newcastle ————————

Mountains and clouds, Luggala

Greystones pier

Tyre specialist, Arklow

Winter, Glenmacnass river

National park tour guides, Glendalough

Gardeners, Powerscourt estate

TO AIMêE ACROSS THE BRIDGE OF LIGHT

The cosmic heat of molten stone, that from creation's forge was
Spat by clashing continents into the limestone beds, and raised
By time to form the granite hills which crest at Lugnaquillia's dome
I here invoke; and all the warmth of July suns that bake the dunes
At Brittas Bay, and turn the sludge grey sea to bright blue shades
And light the gloomy Wicklow coasts and heads with golden fire
I gather in my palm

The purest springs that spurt in threads from Wicklow's rocky core
To feed the ancient holy wells, and tears that fall from angry clouds
In floods to fuel the steep rimmed valleys' falls and bubbling streams
I here invoke; and all the furious motion of the Dargle's rushing gorge,
The stillness of unfathomed mountain tarns and cliff-girt basin lakes,
And Poulaphooca's haunted shores and long-drowned pasturelands
I gather in my palm.

The fertile soils that clothe in green the glens' deep floors and fields
And fed the herds of giant-tined elk at Glenmacnass in ages gone,
Then birthed Coollatin's woods, the last of Wicklow's fabled oaks,
I here invoke; And peaty gleys where gorse and wildflowers turn
The black bog bright, and pastures where fat cows and bullocks
Graze with sheep, and horses step like kings upon the grassy thrones
I gather in my palm.

The scything winds and nameless breezes of the busy Wicklow air
That from all compass points caress or pound the hedgerowed fields,
And drive the ravenous tides in waves against the crumbling cliffs
I here invoke; and mild Saharan gusts that drop grey desert sand
Upon the Springtime grass, and Greenland's freezing winter teeth,
And harsh Atlantic gales and shivered whispers from Siberian wastes
I gather in my palm.

These essences, and what I've heard from Wicklow's deepest soul
Of stony fields and Famine years and the Tudors' raids and wars,
And all the hardness and potential pain that made her children strong
I gather in my palm; and firmly pressed into a ball I hurl with prayer
Across the arching firmament upon a bridge of light - and here invoke
The healing powers of Fire and Water, Earth and Air upon your head
To stop the tumor's growth.

David Pritchard © 1999

Liam Blake was born in Dublin and his photography for Real Ireland Design was responsible for a new style of Irish postcard. He is the author of several photographic books and his work is known world wide through the Real Ireland post-card, calendar, book and poster ranges.